The Fox on the Roundabout

Gareth Owen was born and raised in Ainsdale, Lancashire, where his main ambition was to play inside forward for Everton and England. He left school at sixteen for the merchant navy but was invalided out after falling from a mast in Buenos Aires.

After various jobs (factory work, bookselling, clerical work) he attended Bretton Hall Training College as a mature student and taught Drama and English in a Secondary Modern School in Ilford before becoming a lecturer at Bordesley College, Birmingham.

There he began to write poems, plays and musicals and also did some acting and directing. He formed a fringe theatre company and for a time he managed the career of soul singer Ruby Turner and ran his own record company.

He reads his own work regularly in schools but also enjoys reciting the work of other writers in colleges and arts festivals up and down the country. He reads regularly for the BBC and for two years presented Radio 4's long-running *Poetry Please*.

He now lives in Ludlow, Shropshire.

'Owen engages with questions of identity, emotional betrayal, unsettling changes of circumstance, love and loss ... These are poems for private reading and long thought ... This book digs deep and strikes lucky.'

Times

The Fox on the Roundabout

POEMS BY
GARETH OWEN

MACMILLAN CHILDREN'S BOOKS

For Beryl and Peter

First published 1995 by Collins Children's Books, a division of
HarperCollins*Publishers* Ltd

This edition published 2002 by Macmillan Children's Books
a division of Pan Macmillan Limited
20 New Wharf Road, London N1 9RR
Basingstoke and Oxford
www.panmacmillan.com

Associated companies throughout the world

ISBN 0 330 48468 0

Text copyright © Gareth Owen 1995

The right of Gareth Owen to be identified as the
author of this work has been asserted by him in accordance
with the Copyright, Designs and Patents Act 1988.

1 3 5 7 9 8 6 4 2

A CIP catalogue record for this book is available from
the British Library.

Typeset by Intype London Ltd
Printed and bound in Great Britain by Mackays of Chatham plc, Kent

Contents

The Fox on the Roundabout

A fox upon our roundabout
Watching Saabs and Volvos pass
Like a fully paid-up member
Of our village middle class.

Oldest son at Sandhurst
Daughter at the Sorbonne
Rarely considered the passing years
Or where his life has gone.

Holiday home in Frinton
Thursdays, a hand of Bezique
Treasurer of the Rotary Club
Eighteen holes each week.

Searched for his pipe in his cardi
Broke a buttercup
Wondered should he mow the lawn
Or help with the washing up.

Death of an Old Footballer

He was ready when the whistle blew
Laced up both his boots
Jumped up smiling from the bench
One of life's substitutes.

Raised his arm to the popular end
Flexed the suspect knee
And out of habit showed his studs
To the eternal referee.

Yeah!

"Let's face it," Spanner said,
"Fame and money
It's not just a myth, right,
It's got to happen somewhere
And to somebody
So why not us?
And why not now?"
Yeah!
So he borrows seventy quid
Off his nan down Chelmsley Wood
To demo this song of Nigel's
On this little four track
In Bob Lamb's in Moseley.
OK, it's a grotty bedroom, yeah,
But it's where UB40 started out
Before they went mega
So there you go.

We laid the rhythm track down first
And though I say it myself
It come over really tasty
With Nige's Fender booming out;
Sort of very 80s, yeah,
But with a touch of Clash in there someplace.

When his turn come round
Spanner found it hard
Keeping time with the click track;
Pretended like he couldn't give a toss

The way he does
But I could see him sweating cobs,
His fingers fumbling in the strings.
But you have to remember, right,
Apart from Nigel
None of us could play till two months back.
But, like Spanner said,
What's a few bum notes
If the energy's right?
Yeah!
And we all punch the air
And dance around till the floor shakes
And an old bloke downstairs
Starts banging on the ceiling.
You have to laugh, eh!

The vocal, right,
Was down to me.
Like Spanner said
I give it loads of welly
And I have to say,
Listening to the playback on the cans
With the reverb touching max,
It really come across.
Spanner was bouncing his head
The way he does, you know,
Clicking his fingers.
Yeah!
Well, why be modest, right?
It sounded really great to me.
But when I clock Nige
He has this look across his face

And I just know he isn't satisfied.
So then I have to do it all again;
And then again!
Ten times!
And still he isn't satisfied.
So in the end
Because we're pushed for time
He gets his sister, Karen,
To double up my track –
"Just to thicken out the sound."

Karen! I mean, she's only fifteen!
Goes to ballet classes
And reads books just for the fun of it.
All right, so she can sing in tune
And read music,
But what does she know
About our kind of sound?
This total energy concept
We're trying to generate?
I told Nige what I thought
But he seemed well-pleased
With the track we'd done;
Said the two voices sounded great
And told me not to worry,
Bob and him would fix it in the mix.
Yeah!

When the Local Radio
Played it that Wednesday night
I couldn't believe me ears.
I was nowhere. I mean nowhere.

All you could hear was Karen.
It just wasn't like our sound at all.
Anyway, this Indie Company
Give us a thousand quid advance
And started putting it about.
So thank you very much.

After Peely played it on his show
We got this write-up in the NME
That Spanner got blown up
In case we got some bookings.
Even Radio One picked up on it
And started giving it air time.
Yeah!
We thought, This is it, right,
It's really going to happen.
But all that happened
Was this ginormous silence.
Yeah!
By this time we'd blown the advance
On a C reg Transit.
Was supposed to take us and the gear
To all these gigs we never had.
Spanner went back to fitting tyres
In Bristol Street like he done before.
Then I heard from Nige –
This is on the Thursday, right –
Some A and R man from EMI
Has only signed their Karen up
On a three-year deal.
Yeah!
Last week her first album.

Charted at twenty with a bullet.
Maybe you heard it, right.
No, I didn't think much to it neither
But there you go.
What really pissed me off
Was that after all we'd done
They wouldn't even use our Band
To do the backing track.
Like Spanner said,
There ain't no Justice
And if there is
Like Fame and Money
It's usually happening
Somewhere out of sight
And in some street
We never walked along.

Name
(After the German of Wilhelm Busch)

When I am old and bent, my dear,
And living all alone
I'll hobble from my little home
And sit upon a stone
And thinking of the days gone by
With stick and trembling hand
I'll trace the letters of your name
In the ever-shifting sand.

All the Sad Young Men

Oh, teacher, please, teacher
Don't beat my tiny hand
The answers to your questions
Swarm through my head like sand.
Numbers roll before my eyes
The words burn holes in me
My brain is locked up like a cage
And they've thrown away the key.

The clerk at the Unemployment
Threw my card in an empty tray
"Got no work for layabouts
Come back another day."
The manager at the shipyard
Kicked me out the door
Didn't like the way I cut my mouth
Didn't like the eyes I wore.

Prime Minister on the TV
Said, "Plenty of work around,"
But when I reached the factory
It was bulldozed to the ground.
I talked to this old lady
She was lying by the fence
I wondered why she bled so much
For only fifty pence.

The magistrate polished her glasses
I cried, "Don't send me away.
Don't whisper to each other
Don't stare at me that way."
The courtroom smells of varnish
The law cuts like a knife
There's something being shoved aside
I think it's called my life.

Oh, Mum and Dad, don't send me
To that cold reformatory
I tried to be someone you could like
But I still came out as me.
Please come up and visit me
The days they pass so slow
Pretend you still both love me
So the other boys won't know.

Asked to see the governor
I didn't like my cell
My poor hands wouldn't stop shaking
My head rang like a bell.
I've carved my name upon the wall
For all the world to see
I read it fifty times a day
To remind myself I'm me.

Oh, doctor who delivered me
Didn't you hear the sound
As you tore me from my mother
And watched my eyes roll round?
Oh, mother, didn't you hear it
As my heart began to knock?
The sound of a steel door closing
And a key inside a lock.

Can We Have
Our Ball Back, Please?

England gave football to the world
Who, now they've got the knack,
Play it better than we do
And won't let us have it back.

Long Jump

The long jumper
Sucks in draughts of air
Through an unseen straw,
Shakes water from his hands
And sways, sways
In the gale only he can feel.
Leaping off the board
He bicycles on air
Never reaching the bank
Before the quick sand
Sucks him down.

Marathon Man

The thin-legged man
Totters through the suburbs
With the other escaped convicts
Past chemists' shops and parked cars.
It does not seem to occur to the passers-by
To inform the authorities of the mass break-out
And some even hand them drinks.
Like all the other prisoners
The thin-legged man
Has a number on his back
So the police can identify him.
But even though he stumbles,
White-faced with weariness,
The pursuing cars
Seem incapable of catching him.

The Relay

This is the scroll
Containing the important message.
Each of us runs
Till he can run no more
Then at last gasp
Passes it on.
Eventually the message
Comes full circle to the sender.
When he reads it aloud
We embrace each other in joy
At the news of our victory.

High Jumper

The high jumper
Incessantly treads
Grapes beneath his heels,
Cools his wrists
In currents of air
And bounces, bounces
In an arc towards the bar
Touching the hot coals
Beneath his feet
As little as possible.

Pet Ducks

The farmer's wife gave them to us
I just couldn't resist;
Well, you wouldn't have been able to either
If you'd been there,
They're that adorable.
Gordon, that's my husband,
He fell for them right away
You know what he's like
With anything small and cuddly,
And I'm the same
As well you know.
Anyway
The first thing we had to do
Was give 'em names.
Gordy called his Brian.
No, I didn't care for it neither
Well, he just didn't look like a Brian to me
You know how you just know.
But Gordon liked it;
He said it suited.
I called mine April.
No, I just thought she was,
Well, so feminine, that's all.
And April was the month we bought them;
Yes I thought that was nice,
Perfect choice I thought.
They were a treat really.
We fed them every day
In this plastic basin we had.

We had to laugh
They were that comical.
You'd have laughed too
If you'd have seen them
Trying to eat and swim.
All at the same time.
Hours of endless entertainment they gave us.
I loved
I just loved to hold them;
Feel their little hearts fluttering.
Beautiful it was
Fair made me cry.
And they'd waddle up to greet us
Waddle, waddle, waddle,
They were that pleased to see us
I'm not joking.
You can tell these things
Well I can anyway.
Hello April, I'd say,
Hello Brian.
They knew us
Oh they knew us all right,
Knew our voices;
Came to our hands.
No, not any more.
Well, we had to let them go.
Got too big in the end, see.
Well, they were eating everything in sight.
That dahlia you gave us last Christmas
Remember with the red petals
Well that went
And the michaelmas daisies.

Everything.
The garden would have been a wilderness
Before you could look round.
Of course we were sad,
Who wouldn't be?
But the farmer said he'd look after them
And I'm sure he will.
No money changed hands
But I could tell by his face,
You can tell sometimes can't you?
Well I can anyway.
They have a proper pond now
Mud, cows, hens and other ducks.
Plenty of company.
They're happy now
Don't you think?
Yes, they're happy.
We go to see them
When Gordy can get away.
We call to them and wave.
I'm sure they hear us.
Course we can't tell which they are now.
But I'm sure they know us.
Don't you think they do?
I think they do
Don't you?

The Green Scarf

Alice in her bedroom
Mummy on the stair
Daddy in the stables
Saddling the bay mare.

Alice sees the lady
Hears her silver laugh
Sees the golden hair caught up
In a grass-green scarf.

Alice at the window
Two riders cross the moat
Sees the green scarf knotted
At her daddy's throat.

Alice in her bedroom
Combs her long black hair
Hears hoofbeats on the driveway
And weeping on the stair.

Overheard

"Going over Dudley Sunday
Have a cup of tea with me nan,"
I overheard the fat man with
I Love Miami
Day-gloed across his cap say
At the IKEA checkout counter.
And in that passing moment
Behind the simple phrase
I saw a lifetime walking
Down an endless street of days.

Gathering in the Days

I saw my grandad late last evening
On a hillside scything hay
Wiped his brow and gazed about him
Gathering in the day.

My grandmother beside the fireplace
Sleeps the afternoons away
Wakes and stirs the dying embers
Gathering in the day.

Heard screams and laughter from the orchard
Saw a boy and girl at play
Watched them turn their heads towards me
Gathering in the day.

And my mother at a window
On some long-forgotten May
Lifts her eyes and smiles upon us
Gathering in the day.

And all the people I remember
Stopped their lives and glanced my way
Shared the selfsame sun an instant
Gathering in the day.

Playing at Dying

She was prepared for dying
Because he'd died before
A hundred times she'd found him
Stiff on the bedroom floor.

He'd fallen out of cupboards
He'd stifled on the mat
He'd drowned in the bath with eyes astare
Struggling like a rat.

He'd slumped to death in the armchair
His hollow eyes remote
He'd choked on the poisoned Horlicks
His hands locked round his throat.

And she but half believing
The game that kept them apart
Begged and cajoled and exhorted
Till her fingers found his heart.

"It's only a game," he'd told her.
"You know I only pretend."
So she waited by the gravestone
For the game to end.

Siesta

Each day at this same hour
He comes to her
His lady of the afternoons.
Behind closed lids she hears the whispering
  brush-strokes
Gathering in the light, the windows and her
  sleeping form.
Her countenance is often in his dreams
But these are things not spoken of.
Outside the room where all this happens
In a splash of sunlight by the kitchen door
A maid trades amorous gossip with the
  gardener's boy
While shelling peas into her wide-spread lap;
A petal falls, someone puts out washing
And in the orchard among oranges
Her husband, whose idea it was,
Tends his bees, his face inside a net.
"I'm working on your mouth," the painter tells
  her.
She does not know his Christian name.
Her shut lids tremble. Just so
She used to close her eyes in childhood
Feigning sleep or death
Then open them in sudden laughter
To see her father's great moon face
Filling the everywhere;
Then later he was further off
And later still an absence

Like a place she took her heart to ache in.
Remembering this, she feels herself
Absorbed into the room
And in the darkness there
Beyond the limits of herself
Senses the painter with his canvas gone away
And lines of curious, reverential strangers
Filing past the open door
To gaze on her
Like one already dead.

Someone Waiting

Someone waiting in that bare chamber
Upright on a ladder chair
At geometric angles to the boards;
A swollen lute at odd ease
Balanced lambent
Against a window seat;
Dressmaking hung along a kitchen table.
Someone is sitting
Composed for expectation
And another's entrance,
Fixing the point
Beyond which there is no going.
The eyes on someone not yet there
Are promises of flowers.
The air sustains her
Hovering like meditation.
She makes this room a harbour,
She makes herself a boat
Beached on shingle
Patient for the sea's call.
Someone is waiting
In that bare chamber
For feet upon the wooden stairs,
For someone bearing stars and rain
To make this place
All places.

The Phantom of the Lake

Last night I rose up from my bed
And walked beside the lake
I saw the pale moon ride the sky
Heard the cold waves break.

A girl stood at my windowsill
Her face gleamed mournfully
A fearful cry rose in her throat
As she turned away from me.

And I wondered if they told her
In the morning by that shore
Of the girl who one day drowned there
A hundred years before.

Street

In the street where I was born
Strangers come and go
Returning after thirty years
There's no one that I know.

Intruders squatting in my home
It's more than I can bear
And beyond the edges of my life
It's happening everywhere.

Kiss and Tell

Squatting in the sunlit gravel
Where the spell first struck
Frogprince sighed a regal, philosophic sigh –
Ho hum. Well there we are, he said,
Deciding then and there
That sang-froid was the order of the day.
Besides, hadn't they warned him countless times
How any untoward excitement
Might one day dam for ever
The silted arteries of his princely heart.
And on balance, he thought to himself,
Taking the long view
The rough with the smooth
Didn't being a live frog
Have it hands down any day of the week
Over being a dead prince.
He thought it did.
Besides, being always up to speed
With all the latest fairy tales
He knew it only required
One lovelorn princess passing by
To plant that magic juicy one
Upon those froggy lips
And Hey Sahazzam!
It's Farewell froggydom
Hello Princey once again
Not to speak of Happy Ever After
Children laughing on the sunlit lawn
And the gleaming Testa Rossa

Crouching on the Royal Drive.
So weighing all things up
Frogprince hunched smiling on his lily pad
Contentedly awaiting his lovely saviour
To dance across the dew
And change his life.

Back at the palace though
Times were hard;
The Palace ballroom and the Counting House
Had both sprung leaks,
The peasantry was muttering and reading books
And down at the drawbridge,
Where the talk was of the Princess
And her body piercing,
Four and twenty bailiffs
Gathered like hunchbacked crows.

Frogprince, of course, knew nought of this.
So when he saw his princess
Prancing pondwards through the moonlight
He fondly reflected,
'Ho hum it's transformation time'
And puckered up.
But alas the golden butterflies
That danced across his lips
Were all too much for him.
The frail paper of his heart
Was ripped to tatters
And back he fell with a froggy plop
Into the pond
And croaked.

Hardly had the ripples settled
Before the Princess,
Swallowing her disappointment
And a green chartreuse,
Was back in the Palace Press Room
Hammering out her exclusive to the world:

Stolen Pondside Date
Of Love Tryst Princess
And Amphibian Lover
Ends in Tragic Death Kiss.

Girl From a Train

We stopped by a cornfield
Near Shrewsbury
A girl in a sun hat
Smiled at me.

Then I was seven
Now sixty-two
Wherever you are
I remember you.

Schoolgirl on a Train

When the girl
I'd never seen before
Who wore the tie
And scarlet uniform
Of the Catholic School
And whose dark eyes
Had almost stopped
The passage of my fifteen-year-old blood
Rose to leave the train
At the station after the golf course
I prayed she'd leave behind
The magazine she read so avidly
So I could read
The selfsame words her eyes had read
And whisper to myself
She read that
She read that
She read that.

Lovesick

I am a schoolgirl sick with love
I mope and gaze at the moon
I don't know who the boy is yet
I hope I meet him soon.

Days at School

Like every day
I open our front door.
Against the creosote fence,
Above the clustering pansies
The roses glow dull red,
And further off
Beyond the maple
And the overgrown canal
The orphan hill
That has no name
Rises to the blue.
Like every morning
I stand in the lay-by
In Penthryn Lane
Waiting for the bus.
Brakes squeal.
Ann, the driver, wears a boiler suit
And works at Revill's garage in the town.
'Remind your mum
To leave me half a dozen eggs,'
She shouts, her eyes upon the road ahead.
Because it's June and hot today
I sit with Kelly at the back
Beside an open window.
She's not my best friend
But you can always talk to her.
The wind that's blown across the Irish sea
And half the breadth of Wales
Before rustling our homework books

And my brown hair
Smells hot today of grass and tar.
Today we're up to Air and Light
In our Jam Jar Science Books.
Later we'll climb on the roof
To drop paper parachutes
On to the playing fields below.
Around the iron gates
The children shout and stare
As we get off the bus.
Next September I'll be at the High School
And someone else
Will sit in my place by the window.
There are stars that die each minute
Before their light comes down to us.
The bell rings
And we crowd shouting
Towards the shadows and the open door.

Bait Poem to Catch Girls

One day
As these things happen
My mind blunt as an old lead pencil
Feeling lonely
Companionless
And what is worse
Without love
I shared myself in a poem
With a girl called Lena
Who did not exist.
To make my despair less
I made her uglier
More companionless than myself;
Lena had cross-eyes
Was flat-chested as a schoolboy
And shared her misery generously.
Studying her I felt better.
Days later
As these things happen
There was a knock upon the door.
At the door
The companionless
Loveless
Cross-eyed
Flat-chested
Misery-sharing girl said,
"I am Lena."
She took off her dress
And for some months

As these things happen
We lived together in some misery.

When she left
I sharpened the lead in my pencil
And wrote about
A beautiful
Companionable
Ripe-chested
Sweet-legged girl
Called Lorna
And waited for the knock upon the door.
As these things happen
I am still waiting
And Lena is thinking of returning.

Sea Song

Who is this
Wading through
The shallows of the sea
Smiling at something
The seabirds have not seen
Singing snatches of forgotten songs
To the wind?
She gathers to her breast
The blades of silver
The moon sheds on water
She plucks from the waves
The flowers that spring
Where her tears have fallen.

Without

Without
The street gleams
Wet with rain
The last red bus has run
The phone is silent
And no letters come.
The long days are raw
With small remembrances
And by night I keep
The corner of the sheet turned back
So that her dreams may enter.

Fate

They told her Love was in the stars
The Future an open door
That if she walked beside the sea
Where she'd never walked before
She'd see her truelove's face appear
In the waves upon the shore.

But what she saw was her own face
White as a sea-drenched bone
And what she heard was the roll of wheels
In the deep sea's monotone
And a carriage with never a window
Drawn by angels carved in stone.

Envelopes and Letters

She felt the shock of love
Was like that moment in a dream
When the whole earth opened up on emptiness
And the falling was for ever
And for ever.

And walking here and there
Down thronging corridors
Among the desks and chairs
She threaded through the other girls
Leaving her silence in the air
Like a scented wake to occupy the space.

And sitting at her desk in History
All unbeckoned, the thought came in
That she was like an envelope
That bore nor name nor destination;
And what she felt was like a letter
The boy had scrawled his name and life upon.
She thought this when the teacher
Questioned her about the dream she occupied
Saying only
Nothing, Miss, nothing,
It's nothing.

Crush

In the second term of the fifth year,
That month we won the Final
Of the Intermediate Cup
And the snow came late
Covering all the playing fields
And heaping up against the Sports Hall,
I came a pearler off my bike
Delivering the *Daily Post*
In Abercrombie Road.
And as I sat there
Deciding if I was alive or dead
This dark-haired girl in a red coat
Jumped off the fifteen bus
And asked me if I was all right.
And alive or dead was not a question any more
Because I've seen this girl before
On Saturdays in Rushworth's
Playing records in a booth
With Pete Almond's sister's cousin
Who's in her class at school
And says she'll fix me up with her
If I'm that desperate.
And Oh, I am, I am that desperate
Because there is no hope
And I am drowning
In those eyes of hers
Those dark grey eyes
That nail my aching heart
And tongue for ever down.

And is this me
My face on fire
Looping the oily chain back on
With streaked and trembling hands,
Walking my buckled bike
Back up the road away from her,
Cursing my coward heart
For all those witty things
I know I could have said
But never did?
And is this me writing
My name and hers together
With an equals in between
In the unbroken snow
Of empty Hesketh Park,
Making a spell against the thaw
They say is bound to come?

Sleeping

Sleeping I'm at my happiest
Morning brings misery
That's when I wake from my dreaming
And remember that I'm still me.

Old Boys' Register

Allendale and Belton and Belvedere and Blunt
Hildyard and Jackson and Johnson and Lunt
Mildwood and Mowbray and Naysmith and Knight
Sineheart and Tildon and Unstead and White.
And Wylde?

Allendale swotted and always came first
Belton had boils that never burst
Belvedere was good at Art
Blunt used to fart.
And Wylde?

Hildyard was sharp and wore loud ties
Jackson took pleasure in torturing flies
Johnson bragged about the girls he'd had
Lunt was mad.
But Wylde?

Mildwood tried to hold your hand
Mowbray buried him in the sand
Naysmith was a useful bat
Knight was fat.
But Wylde?

Sinehart said he didn't care
Tildon who was never there
Unstead sang the latest hits
White had fits.
Was Wylde the one who smiled to himself?

And now:
Allendale runs his father's store
Belton apparently studied law
Belvedere's a diplomat in Spain
Blunt's insane.
Did Wylde sit by the window?

Hildyard is something in the States
Jackson sells brooms round housing estates
Johnson married a wealthy bride
Lunt died.
But Wylde?

Mildwood went to teach abroad
Mowbray is a rep with Ford
Naysmith wandered far and wide
Knight tried.
And Wylde?

Sineheart surprised us by flying high
Tildon's researching for ICI
Unstead demos enamel sinks
White drinks.
And Wylde took a shotgun and blew out the brains
    of his three children.

Gold

"Where do you get your ideas from?"
The children often ask.
And I tell them the old old tale:
How it's no good
Sitting on your bum at home
Waiting for lightning to strike
Or the parcel post
To bring the polished ingots
To your door.
No. This is more how it goes:
Knock the dirt off your spade,
Set out for the hills
And get to digging.
Another thing:
Ever since I first began
I've had the idea
That the finished article
Lies smiling doggo and complete somewhere
Just waiting to be found,
Like the young king's golden effigy
Carter dug out at Sumra.

Most days of course
All you come up with
Is a pile of broken stones.
But better stones, I say,
Than buckets full of air.
At least you can build yourself a cairn
To prove you once passed by.

Yes, that's the main thing,
That and a working knowledge
Of the layout of the land.
Oh, and of course a serviceable spade
That knows how to strike lucky
From time to time.

The Last Tiger

Soon there will be no more of us;
I am the last of all my tribe.
Here I wait, O my father,
My fangs rotted to stumps and black blood
Amongst the clapboard hovels of the suburbs.
Here I wait, O my sons who never were,
In the days of my dying,
The gunshot festering in my hollow side,
Filling my belly on the wind.
Here I wait, O my ancestors,
Amongst the tin cans and the dustbins,
Gnawing at my broken paw,
The kingdom of my spirit
Shrunk to a white-hot tip of hate.
Here I wait, O my cousins,
To kill this old woman
Who will limp across the cinders
With two buckets in her hands.

But I have a dream, O my gods,
I have a dream
That shuts out the hunger and the dying;
I have a dream,
That in my ancient, burning strength
I will roam the ancient cities of mankind
And, screaming, claw the stolen coats
Of you, my honoured sisters and brothers
From the backs of rich and beauteous ladies.
Thus, do not ask me why I hate women.

Traveller

Where are you going to, walking, walking?
And what is in your pack?

I'm travelling to an unknown land
With my years upon my back.

And what do you hope to find there?
And will you find a bed?

I'll find me a bank of sweet dark earth
And pull it over my head.

Dad

Two days before he died
My sister made a bed for him
In what they called his living room.
Too busy chasing every breath by now
The irony passed him by.
On the TV in the corner
Two ageing gunslingers
Challenged each other
To one last shoot-out
Before a paying audience
In the sand-strewn bullring.
"Winner takes all," snarled Kirk,
But what the winner takes, I thought,
Is what we all of us will get
If we wait unchallenged long enough.

They never said that in those
Happy Ever After films
We once were nourished on,
That always faded in impassioned kisses.
But in the streets outside
Hurrying homewards to our several lives
We soon find out the *After's* not for *Ever*
And even star-kissed lips
Dissolve to dust in Time.

Westerns he'd always liked
But this last one outlived him
So he never saw the final

Thundering shoot-out in the sun,
Nor heard the diapason swell
Above the closing titles
And the last dissolve.

Punctilious to the last,
Sensing an appointment to be kept,
He wound his watch a final time,
Told Anne he loved her,
Then composed himself until
The erratic knocking in his wrist
Gave up the ghost for good.
Someone opened a window
For his fleeing soul
And across the hills
The great and endless night
Came pouring in from everywhere.

Hamlet

Well, he had something of your height,
Compact, I'd say, but by no means slight;
Approachable, certainly, although patrician,
But with something dangerous in his disposition;
A passion wedded to urbanity,
A kind of elegant barbarity
That many others found attractive.
An intellect that was speculative
Rather than analytic. Fond of the stage
And skilful with the foils as any of his age.
Sat a horse well, knew how to dress,
Drank a little, swore, but never to excess –
At least not that I heard tell
But then I never knew him quite as well
As many you could ask. A student tends
To gravitate to exclusive groups of friends
And so it was with me. The last
I saw of him was when his carriage passed
My college window. He had to leave
Quite suddenly for Elsinore,
I never quite found out what for;
Trouble in the family I believe.

The Visitor

Jesus came today
Filling the square of light
From the open door.
Presence he certainly had
And much more reality
Than the pictures we had seen
Had led us to expect.
Dignity he had of course
But one understood
How the nails battered
Through the splintering palms
Must have agonised.
Surprisingly our concern
Was with trivialities:
Would his humility
Accept the distinction
Of our best cloth?
And me disturbed
About the ambiguity
Involved in the simple act
Of washing my hands.

And Did You Once See Georgie Best
(After Browning)

And did you once meet Georgie Best
And did you take his photograph?
What did he look like? Did he speak?
Did you get his autograph?

When I was five I saw him play
Sitting on my father's knee
I shouted out his name and waved
Did he, I wonder, mention me?

The Good Handyman's Guide to Fantasy

Now in those far off days
When Gutter Drip the Dragon Slayer
Still walked the harsh land
Of Downpipe Overlap Bolted Together,
Which lay between the mountain of Spindlewasher
And the mighty ocean of Upper Sash,
Word came wind-borne
From the Kingdom of that greatest of Lords,
Whom men call Archetrave Door Sag,
That in the night when no stars shone
The great dragon Screed Batten Wall Render,
He of the mitred corners and the bare-faced tenon,
Bearing on his back his master
That most treacherous necromancer
Ridge Tile Slaters Ripper
Took up the sleeping forms
Of Archetrave Door Sag's two daughters;
Bracket For Half Round Guttering,
Of whose beauty
The like has not been seen
Since the world first breathed,
And her younger sister
Inspection Trap Screw Plunger.
And these two maids the monster bore from thence
Upon the spiny ridges of his dragon back
To that shadowy, fearful cavern
That lies between the peaks

Of Rebate Hanger Hinge
Which Ridge Tile Slaters Ripper
Called his home.

Now when Archetrave Door Sag
Heard the fateful tidings
He was sore peeved
And fell forthwith into a state
Of frittering indecisiveness
And weeping called out to his people saying:
"Listen my people, for it is I
Archetrave Door Sag who speaks."
And his people replied with one great voice,
"We know that already."
And Archetrave Door Sag
Drew from its stone scabbard
The great and shimmering blade
That men call Mantelpiece Surround
And waving it thrice
About his grey and grizzled locks
Raised his voice once more and said,
"Which one of you now, O my warriors,
Will venture forth alone
To the land of Rebate Hanger Hinge
And challenge there in battle on to death
Screed Batten Wall Render
And his master the necromancer
Ridge Tile Slaters Ripper
Under the blood-red sky of
Downpipe Overlap Bolted Together
And bring back to my bosom
My two fair daughters,

Bracket For Half Round Guttering
And my youngest, my beloved
Inspection Trap Screw Plunger
Whose eyes are of the hue
Of Hessian Webbing Rubber,
Who will do this?"
And when they heard this tearful plea
Each man assembled there stepped forth
And with one voice cried out:
"Him, him."

Now when he heard this
Lord Archetrave Door Sag
Turned to his most faithful servant
Hose Pipe Wire Bending
And in a whisper,
So that his voice was like on to
Wind that hath long lain trapped,
Said: "Hose Pipe Wire Bending
Most loyal of Men
Seek you out the warrior
Gutter Drip Dragon Slayer
And charge him with this task.
And tell him for reward
He shall have as bride
The virgin hand
Of whomsoever of my daughters
Shall please him best.
Tell him this."

Ten long and bitter years elapsed
'Ere Hose Pipe Wire Bending,
His hair now white with toil and pain,
Limped nigh to death
Back to the castle of Archetrave Door Sag.
But 'ere yet one word of what he knew
Could quit those ancient wrinkled lips
He waved a paper in the air
And groaning fell from off his steed
Where Yeoman Death, who waits upon us all,
Bore him swift away
To that far land men call
Stop Cock.

And Archetrave Door Sag
Plucked up the paper that erstwhile
Fell from Hose Pipe Wire Bending's hand
And read aloud the fateful words
That Gutter Drip had written there:
Sorry, I'm not available at the moment
Please leave your name and message
And I'll get back to you
As soon as possible
Thank you.

Stranger in the House

I have entered the wrong house again!
Creeping from room to room I wonder
Where are my carpets and my chairs,
My family photographs, my books,
My watercolours done by hand?
Even the smell is different.

A strange dog bounds panting down the stairs
And slobbers his affection on my hand.
And then these children
I have never seen before
Call me their father
Clutch my hand and laughing
Crawl upon my knee.

And who is this tall woman
Who greets me with a kiss
Laying cool hands upon my face
And whispering in my ear
Sweet names I've never heard before?
And when alone at last
I face my bedroom glass
Some shifty, callow counterfeit
Stares back at my discomfiture.

No, I have certainly entered
The wrong house again.
Tomorrow something must be done.
But the habits of a lifetime
Are hard to break.

Silent Poem

*(4' 33" is the title of a piece for any instrument
by John Cage. It consists of the performer sitting
in silence for the stipulated time.)*

Please listen carefully:
In what follows
The terms *poem* and *silence*
Shall be taken to be synonymous and
   interchangeable.
The silences we shall be concerned with
Shall be those silences we shall be concerned with
And none other.
Please be on the alert for imitations.
For what we are gathered here to observe
Is an absence; a non existence.
I repeat, non existence.
It is important therefore
That you remain seated;
Do not, I repeat, not leave the room.
Were we all to do so
There would be nobody here
To observe the existence of this non existence.
I cannot impress upon you too seriously
How grave such a case would be.
If however your departure proves unavoidable
Please do so with the minimum of fuss.
To facilitate this
Please observe now your nearest exit point,
Plan your route in advance,
Move silently. Walk, don't run.

The words.
Between the silences will be words.
The words however are not the poem.
They exist merely to draw our attention to the
    silences.
Those at the beginning
Indicate the imminence of the silence.
Those at the end
Indicate that the silence is concluded.

Should you, by some chance,
Hear silences other than those
With which we are concerned
There is no cause for agitation.
You are undergoing
A species of religious experience known
    commonly as
Not hearing voices.
Joan of Arc did not suffer from this.
Thank you for your attention
When all is ready I shall begin.

I'm sorry that was not the poem
I repeat not the poem.
That silence was mistaken.
Those of you who believe it was a poem
Erase it from your memory.
Here is the poem.

Someone made a sound.
The silence could not make itself heard.
I shall therefore read the poem again.

Here is an encore.

Here is the poem backwards.

This is the poem read more slowly.

Here is the poem sideways.

Here is the poem translated into Welsh.

This time all join in the chorus.

You may take this poem home with you.
When you are feeling tired
Recite it to yourself thus.

It can be obtained
On any wave of your radio.
Simply turn the on/off switch
To the *off* position.

There it was again.
If you should choose
To recite it in public
Please pay your royalties promptly.
On this occasion as you listen
Analyse the rhyme scheme.

Finally here is the poem once more
In its original form.

Aaaaaaaaaaaaagh!
Do not be alarmed
That was not the poem expressing pain.
Silence is of its nature silent
And suffers without complaint.
This has its dangers
For like a body which registers no pain
It may extinguish itself unobserved.
Remember that
The next time you break it.

Up at the Farm

Margaret's dad's a widower and farms
Seven stony acres up the beck at Oringham.
Each Sunday afternoon
I cycle up from our estate
To where she sits awaiting me
Upon the broken wooden gate.
She takes me up the slope
Behind the grey stone house
And there we gather up
Amongst the pear and apple trees
The nestling eggs
The hens lay anywhere.

Each winter her dad buys in
A dozen long-lashed calves
To fatten up for Easter sales.
Out of their slaughter,
With what she calls
Her Beast Money,
She gets each year a brand-new coat.
For this I envy her
And for the curtain
Of thick and creamy hair
That swings about her shoulders and her throat.

She says:
"Nine years ago today
My mam collapsed and died.
I can't remember her at all

But Daddy says she used to dust
The cottage *every* day
And then on Thursday, without fail,
Move all the furniture around."

At table her father
Hardly says a word
But drinks his tea bolt upright
Staring at the wall behind my head.
His eyebrows gather in a frown
At every squeaking chair
Or when a knife or fork
Chimes on a salad plate.
I hear my own throat swallowing.

I see a baby, on a cushion,
Playing with her feet;
A young man sits upright
Before the kitchen range,
His hands between his knees.
And in the room's still centre
A woman lies upon the floor;
She has Margaret's hair
And the dust drifts down
Into her open mouth;
Drifts across the tables,
The sofas and the stacks of chairs
That stand about her
Where they last were left,
Like bumper cars abandoned
When the music had to stop.

Institution Annie

Institution Annie
Occupies a daze
The hours taste like breadcrumbs
The long years pass like days.

Keeps the face of the mirror
Turned towards the screen
Eighty-seven on the outside
Within she's still seventeen.

Sister gives her the mirror
And she hides her head in disgrace
Says to herself: "Oh Annie,
What have they done to your face?"

Icarus

Icarus
Spat out by sun
As fly from cat's mouth
Fell through dimensions of eternity
Danced the idiot's dance
Down broken rungs of sky
Discharged his senses on the stars
The screaming was outside himself
Ears baring teeth
Tore up his scalp
Eyes crawled on his face
Hooked out by windy claws
The sea crashed up
With scales of fire
Earth was upside down
Death's hand wrenched his hair
Dragging him through tunnels of agony
World rolled in his bowels
Inside was out
Felt the sea
Like spikes of rock
Crack his bones
Spring his ribs
Spread his lungs on red water
His nature
Cracked by air and sea
Buoyed belly up
Fell open
Like the secret of a flower

Like a rose in a wheel of foam
Sent petals spinning outward
Tremors of blood
To the world's edge.

Icarus by Mobile

Daddy, Daddy is that you?
Listen I don't have much time OK
But I wanted to say, right
It's back to the drawing board, Daddy
The whole contraption is a no no.
The wings?
No, the wings worked fine
Couldn't fault the wings in any way
The wings were ace
And your calculations on the stresses
Re wind and feathers
Spot on!
Likewise the pinion tolerances
And remember that flap factor
That gave us both such sleepless nights
Let me tell you
Those flaps worked like a dream
But Daddy
Oh, Daddy
How could you forget the sun!
You told me?
What is this 'I told you!'
I don't have much time
So listen OK
We're talking equations here
Just let me spell it out for you:
Solar heat + bees' wax + ambition =
Total Meltdown and I mean total
Which equals to put it simply

Your boy Icarus on collision course
With something called the Earth.
Daddy, I don't have much time
Let me give you my co-ordinates
For the pick-up
OK stretch of headland and a bay
Visibility good outlook calm. And hey
Am I lucky
Or am I lucky!
There's a galleon anchored near the shore
Looks like Icarus
Is in for an early pick-up this fine morning.
And over there some poor old farmer's
Ploughing through a field of stones
And here's an old boy with a fishing pole and
Listen, Daddy
Would you believe
Some guy just out of frame
Is painting the whole thing.
And now I'm waving, Daddy, waving
Any minute now they'll all look up and
So listen, Daddy, I don't have much time
I'm going to start screaming soon OK?
Can you still hear me?
I don't have much
Daddy, I just wanted to ask
You know
About my mum
Was she
Listen Daddy
I don't have much time
I

An Attempt at the Shortest Poem in the World

Already
This is too long.

Country Singer's Lament

I made a million singing love songs
Got two wives chasing me,
They live in Hope and Bitterness
I live in Tennessee.

The Ballad of the Waltzing Kid

It was quiet as a grave that Saturday
Nuthin' moved in the town's Main Street
'Cept fer a drunk falling down by the Last Chance
  Saloon
And a dawg snappin' flies in the heat.

Matt Streicher, the marshall, smoked a black cheroot
His face was as hard as his gun
He wore a dirty black patch over one good eye
While the other one smiled at his son (that was
  Billy).

Young Billy and him was crackin' a bottle
Playin' five card stud
Matt ruled that town on fear and graft
And his story was written in blood.

It was Billy who saw the stranger first
Silhouetted against the sun
Dressed head to foot in a broadcloth suit
And on his hip gleamed a gun.

He whistled a tune then he got off his horse
Then he waltzed his way over the floor
Then he waltzed in a circle, ordered a drink
And stood there ready to draw.

A whisper ran round The Last Chance Saloon
When they saw the dance that he did
And the whisper grew till it spelled out the name
Of the man they called The Waltzing Kid.

Young Billy's heart beat faster
When he heard the stranger's name
Like many a greenhorn dude before
He saw his chance for fame.

The Waltzing Kid spoke quiet and slow
Said, 'Don't nobody give me no lie
I'm lookin' fer a man, I don't know his name
But I know he has one yellow eye.'

Said Billy: 'Kid I heard 'bout you'
And his voice rang mockingly,
'F' you really are the Waltzing Kid
Let's see you waltz fer me.'

The Kid's blue eyes were chips of ice
He said, 'Son, just git outta town
I don't have no quarrel with you
Don't make me shoot you down.'

Now Billy was know to have a fast draw
Maybe the fastest in the land
But the Kid was so fast no one saw him move
Just the smoking gun in his hand.

As Billy slumped down to the sawdust
He heard a tune sweet and low
Saw the high-heeled boots of the Waltzing Kid
Dance slow-slow-quick-quick-slow.

'Shall I tell you why I dance?' said the Waltzing Kid
And the men gathered round to hear
And Marshall Streicher he lifted the patch
So he could see the stranger clear.

'My ma met Pa in a dance hall
Hadn't seen a girl in five years
And Ma was so took with his fancy steps
They banished her maidenly fears.

'And Pa found his mountain man passion
Was more than warmly received
And it was there while the band played the
   Thanksgivin' Waltz
That the Waltzing Kid was conceived.'

Matt Streicher moved closer and closer
And if anyone'd looked they'd have seen
That the eye the patch kept hidden
Was hard and yellow and mean.

But the Kid he saw that eye clear
For a second his face turned pale
Then a strange kind o' smile lit up his face
And he carried on with his tale.

''Bout nine months later I was set to be born
Ma and Pa they went out dancin' again
But a yellow-eyed man saw them laughing and
    waltzing
Who had once loved Ma in vain.

'When he saw Ma aloving why he leapt to his feet
With a six gun in every hand
Said, "If I can't have you to be my wife
Then neither will no other man."

'Well Pa tried to calm old Yellow Eye
But before he had time to protest
A shot runged out, Ma gave a shout
And she fell down clutching her breast.

'She had flunged herself forward protectin' Pa
She give her life (which was all that she'd got)
But the bullet passed through her, came out the back
And killed Pa with the very same shot.

'Well, the shock of the dyin' was too much fer Ma
But before she passed away
She give birth to me right there on the floor
While the band continued to play.

'So
I was born and conceived to the strains of a waltz
And Ma with her very last sigh
Said, "Son, when you're a man take vengeance upon
The man who has one yellow eye." '

The Kid said to Streicher who was stealin' off,
'You can run or you can stay
Makes no difference to me, Matt Yellow Eye
This gun's gonna blow you away.'

Two shots rung out at the very same time
And through the smoke and the din
Matt Streicher lay adyin' with a hole in his head
Where his one yellow eye had bin.

But the Waltzing Kid had been shot in the back
Young Billy had played him false
And as he slid down to the spitoons and the dust
The band played the Gunfighter's Waltz.

The Kid forgive Billy with his very last breath
While the band played sweet and low
And his feet as they twitched in a dance of death
Went slow-slow-quick-quick-slow.

And they say on some nights when the stars shine
   bright
And the wolves howl forlorn at the moon
A man dressed in black with a gun on his hip
Waltzes slow through the Last Chance Saloon.

Hound Dog and Heartbreak

Must've been in me pram
When I heard them all first time round:
Hound Dog and *Mystery Train*,
Heartbreak Hotel
And *Blue Moon of Kentucky*.
So you might say the King was in my blood.
At eight I'd sing along to the Dansette
Hitting the poses for the bedroom mirror
The legs going haywire
Strumming the broken racket
And the old fella screaming up the stairs,
"Shut up yer bleeding row for God's sake."

At fourteen I started shaving,
Thickened out the sideburns with Mam's pencil,
Brylcreamed the pompadour
And locked the sneer in permanent
With a paperclip by night.
But things really started to take off
When I come equal second, highly commended
In the Elvisly Yours Look Alike Contest;
Three girls screamed and made me
Autograph their arms with lipstick,
And I kissed Tina behind The Grapes
That never-to-be-forgotten October night.
It was all for the King
But I felt this tide of fame
Beckoning to me from afar.

On Jan 8th '69, His birthday,
I changed my name to you-know-what by deed poll
And me and Tina started shacking up.
I was working in accounts
For Metal Box back then,
Not what He'd have done I know
But every penny I could save
Was all for Elvis and the Dream.
It started with the white karate suits
The silk cloak and the diamantés.
Then we had the pillars
Erected out the front
And the whole upstairs
Done out like Graceland.
The place was like a shrine.
People came from miles
To Capon Road to stand and stare
And *Midlands Today* come down
And did this interview
With me in all me gear.
Worked all the hours God sent me
To make the payments on the nose
The transplant and the lips.
Tina couldn't stand it in the end:
"I don't know who I'm sleeping with no more,"
She screamed and took off for her mum's
Taking little Elvis with her.
She didn't understand,
Women don't, do they?
I was gutted something rotten
But at least I understood
What He'd gone through

When that Priscilla walked out on him.

Don't want to talk about
What happened in '77.
I tell you it near finished me.
Don't open the door to nobody no more;
Only go out to pick the giro up.
To help the swelling in me legs
I sit in the bath for hours some nights
Eating cream cakes and supping lager.
The plug hole's clogged with hair
And the silence is something else.
Wednesday I put an advert in the *Mail*;
Old Hound Dog is Lonesome Tonight
At the Heartbreak Hotel.
Vacancies. Call any time.

Bird

Something fluttered about my heart
Like a bird caught in a snare
I blame the girl on the fourteen bus
It was she who put it there.

Tortoise

There's a tortoise in our classroom
We sit at the back of the class
Both gazing out of the window
Watching the slow hours pass.

There's a tortoise in our classroom
Miss Kent lets me keep him there
To prove how the slow and the dreamy
Can sometimes outrun the hare.

Blind Date

You are who I think you are, aren't you?
I thought you were.
You had that look
Pick you out a mile.
Bucks Fizz will do me fine.
Look, you won't mind will you
If I get something off my chest?
Well, I don't want you to take this personally
But I don't think much of men.
If you'd known my ex
You'd feel the same.
No, not hate exactly;
He didn't have the character
To be someone you could hate –
I resented that in him.
No, it was just that he was
A slimy, spineless, two-timing bastard
Who thought I was too stupid
To know what was going on
Between him and that Linda
Whatsername down in Graphics.
Apart from that he was perfect.
Even had the cheek to introduce me to her
At the staff and wives shindig that Christmas.
I felt sorry for her really.
Well, you'd feel sorry for anybody
Who thought my Barry was wonderful.
I thought it would fizzle out
But it didn't. So in the end

I did my big confrontation bit.
'Course, he puts on this innocent
Who, me? look.
But his eyes were all over the place.
Yes, I'll have another, thanks.
Does it bother you if I smoke?
It does some.

What was I saying?
Oh yes, like I said
He tried to deny it;
Said it had been Linda's fault
She'd been all over him from the start,
Wouldn't leave him alone
Or take no for an answer.
I was the only one he really loved,
I had to believe him.
Then he starts crying. Real tears.
He thought that would make it all right.
Pathetic! "What about me, Barry?" I said.
"What about my tears?"
What do men know about crying?
Where weeping's concerned
I'm the world's expert.
He said it was all over between them.
I told him, it had better be
Or he wouldn't see the house,
The BMW or the kids again.
That really put the frighteners on him.

So, we were all right for a bit.
I got this promotion at Jackson's:

Area Sales, Roller Blinds.
It's very interesting really.
What do you do?
Oh, I see, that must be nice.
Anyway, three months after all this
He comes to me with this sad story
How Linda's three months gone
By this spotty Herbert in Dispatch
Who's still wet behind the ears
And everywhere else by all accounts.
He said he just felt sorry for her
She being just eighteen and everything,
Her mum and dad were Jehovah's Witnesses
And were going to chuck her out,
Couldn't we put her up for a few months?
Just till everything quietened down.
I said to him straight
I said: "Barry, tell me the truth.
It is all over with you and her, isn't it?"
He said: "What sort of man d'you think I am?
D'you think I'd lie to you?"
I didn't answer that.
Am I talking too much?
Just stop me if I do.
Anyway, like a fool, I let her stay.
That Friday she moved in with us
And we gave her the room in the back.
Got on all right too I must say.
She was good with Philippa and Mark.
It was really nice as well
Having another woman around the place.
She even started decorating the bedrooms.

Then one afternoon
I had this call from Head Office,
Someone had let them down
At the last minute
Could I go and demo these New Age roller
    blinds
At the Broad Street Conference Centre?
I'd only got as far as Harbone
When I suddenly realised
I'd left the costings and some samples
In the boot of Barry's car.
They can't have heard the Astra in the drive.
Frankly, I'm not surprised the noise she was
    making.
They heard the door though.
I heard this desperate whispering
And rustling in our room.
When I went up they'd tried to cover up the
    bed;
Said they were decorating.
I don't know if I cried.
I didn't want to in front of her.
You know what really hurt?
She was even wearing that kimono
Barry bought at Rackham's for our tenth.
I just walked out,
Went to my mum and dad's.
Something cracked inside me.
For a year I didn't go out of the house;
I didn't see the kids,
Lost the job of course.
I didn't care to be honest,

Didn't seem to care about anything.
It was like I dried up inside.

Then one afternoon
I was walking in this bit of garden
They have out the back
And heard someone laughing in the greenhouse.
My dad was standing there all tears
Leaning on the water butt
This insect sprayer in his hand.
His cap had fallen on the floor.
He put his arms around me
And I felt his tears all down my neck.
I felt that terrible.
I thought, if my old dad
Can cry for me like that,
I must have been some use
To someone once upon a time.
The next day I went
And started circling likely jobs in red.

And now I'm here. A new woman.
No I'll get these.
You haven't said much.
You're not the quiet type, are you?
I hope you're not deep.
Oh, that's good,
I don't trust people who're deep.
Can I ask you something?
D'you mind?
No, it's just that I was wondering,
What's your favourite Bros record?

The Gift

He's waiting for me when I wake
In the shadows on the stair
In the classroom and the yard
He's waiting for me everywhere.

He gives me blows and lashing words
I give him silence and my cries
And from this bargain something grows
A twisted friendship made of lies.

And there is nowhere I can hide
For even when we're miles apart
He haunts the pillow where I lie
Nursing the bruises of my heart.

And when they ask me for his name
My tongue's a stone, my eye a tear
But in my skull I hear him cry,
"Your name is Victim, mine is Fear!"

And after, though he'd left that place
The fear he'd planted in me grew
So now I'm standing on the stair
To pass it on to someone new.

Index of First Lines

Acknowledgements

Siesta was first published in *With a Poet's Eye* (1986) The Tate Gallery. It's based on a painting by John Frederick Lewis – 'The Siesta'.

The Last Tiger was first published privately in *Salford Road* in 1976 and in *Worlds Apart*, Mary Glasgow Publications Ltd 1987.

Days at School was first published in *Signal Magazine*, September 1991.

Icarus by Mobile was first broadcast by Radio 4 in 1996 and published by Hodder and Stoughton.

Blackbird Has Spoken

Selected Poems for Children by Eleanor Farjeon
Chosen by Anne Harvey

Blackbird Has Spoken is a brand-new selection
of Eleanor Farjeon's poetry which will delight
readers of all ages.

A Morning Song
For the First Day of Spring

Morning has broken
Like the first morning,
Blackbird has spoken
     Like the first bird.
Praise for the singing!
Praise for the morning!
Praise for them, springing
     From the first Word.

Mine is the sunlight!
Mine is the morning
Born of the one light
     Eden saw play
Praise with elation,
Praise every morning
Spring's re-creation
     Of the First Day!

Eleanor Farjeon

Let Me Touch the Sky

Selected poems for children by Valerie Bloom

Let Me Touch the Sky is a brand-new selection of Valerie Bloom's warm, sparky and evocative poetry which will delight readers of all ages.

Autumn Gilt

The late September sunshine
Lime green on the linden leaves
Burns bronze on the slated roof-tops,
Yellow on the farmer's last sheaves.

It flares flame-like on the fire hydrant,
Is ebony on the blackbird's wing,
Blue beryl on the face of the ocean,
Glints gold on the bride's wedding ring.

A sparkling rainbow on the stained-glass window,
It's a silver sheen on the kitchen sink,
The late September sunshine
Is a chameleon, I think.

Valerie Bloom

The Works

*Every kind of poem you will ever need for
the Literacy Hour
Chosen by Paul Cookson*

The Works really does contain every kind of poem you
will ever need for the Literacy Hour but it is also a
book packed with brilliant poems that will delight any
reader.

It's got chants, action verses, riddles, tongue twisters,
shape poems, puns, acrostics, haikus, cinquains,
kennings, couplets, thin poems, lists, conversations,
monologues, epitaphs, songs, limericks, tankas,
nonsense poems, raps, narrative verse and performance
poetry and that's just for starters.

It features poems from the very best classic and modern
poets, for example:

William Blake, Michael Rosen, Robert Louis
Stevenson, Allan Ahlberg, W. H. Auden, Brian Patten,
Roger McGough, Roald Dahl, Charles Causley,
Eleanor Farjeon, Benjamin Zephaniah, Ted Hughes,
T. S. Eliot and William Shakespeare to name but a few.

A book packed with gems for dipping into time and
time again.

All the Things I See

Selected Poems for Children by Jenny Joseph

All the Things I See brings all Jenny Joseph's
wonderfully evocative poems for children together in
one volume for the first time.

Towards the End of Summer

Cherry red and honey bee
Buzzed around the summer flowers
Bumbled round the luscious fruits.
Patient weaver clambered by.

Silently while the others bobbed
And busied in the bright blue air.
Hither, zither, merrily,
Weaver waved his cool brown arms
And gently drew around the tree
Silken skeins so fine so fine
No one could see that they were there,
Until one autumn morning when
Cherry was gone and bee asleep
A silver shawl was laced across the grass
With little beads like pearls strung all along.

Jenny Joseph

Another Day on Your Foot and I Would Have Died

Poems by John Agard, Wendy Cope, Roger McGough, Adrian Mitchell and Brian Patten

Five fabulous poets put their best foot forward and invite you to dip your toes into a wonderful collection of poetry.

I found my sock
beneath the bed.
'Where have you been
all week?' I said.

'Hiding away,'
the sock replied.
'Another day on your foot
and I would have died!'

Roger McGough

A selected list of poetry books available from Macmillan

The prices shown below are correct at the time of going to press. However, Macmillan Publishers reserve the right to show new retail prices on covers which may differ from those previously advertised.

All Macmillan titles can be ordered at your local bookshop or are available by post from:

**Book Service by Post
PO Box 29, Douglas, Isle of Man IM99 1BQ**

Credit cards accepted. For details:
Telephone: 01624 675137
Fax: 01624 670923
E-mail: bookshop@enterprise.net

Free postage and packing in the UK.
Overseas customers: add £1 per book (paperback)
and £3 per book (hardback).